MW00986759

AMAZON DOMINATION

Product Launch Strategy

EcomCrew
THE MULTIMILLION DOLLAR SELLERS
MICHAEL JACKNESS AND DAVE BRYANT

Dedicated to all of the ecommerce wantrepreneurs and entrepreneurs looking to build sustainable ecommerce brands.

Table of Contents

Message from the Crew

Thank you for taking the time to view our Amazon Launch Strategy. The launch strategy that we are about to introduce to you has been used by ourselves to launch countless products to immediate success. Getting initial traction for products is one of the hardest things when launching new products and using this strategy you can overcome this challenge. Along with helping you to launch new products, we'll also help to guide you through the process of vetting products before you commit substantial money to making a large order for them.

The best part about our Launch Strategy is that it's a completely white hat system. It won't put your Amazon account or listings in jeopardy. At EcomCrew we continuously stress the importance of building long term, sustainable businesses and not just using the latest trick or gimmick for short term success.

This Launch Strategy that we are about to present can be used in its entirety or you can pick and choose the elements which are most applicable to you and your products. Regardless of how fully you employ the strategy, our goal is for it to help you launch products with quicker success and reach sales heights you haven't previously.

Happy selling,
Mike & Dave

Introduction

You probably already know about this "magic money machine" that is Amazon.

It's a little bit of an exaggeration, we admit, but if it's the first time you've heard of such a thing and you're dubious (or if you've only associated Amazon with buying stuff), let us paint you a couple of word pictures of how your life may look like if you find success on Amazon:

1. You're employed and you have supplementary income coming from a side hustle selling stuff on Amazon. You don't need to take a second job in order to make ends meet.
2. You have a couple of profitable products selling well on Amazon so you quit your job and still make good money. You have more time to be around your family or to just do the things you always wanted to do.
3. You hire a couple of full-time employees, lease a warehouse and an office, and build a sizeable ecommerce company with Amazon as a major channel.
4. You want to try out the 4-hour workweek lifestyle so you hire a bunch of VAs, automate most of your Amazon business, pack your stuff up and travel the world.

Looks great right? What if we tell you that word pictures 2 and 3 are our reality? We also know a lot of people--personal friends, people from the industry, and EcomCrew students--who live these word pictures as their realities, so maybe "magic money machine" might not be that much of an exaggeration after all.

There's just one problem:

People have been catching up.

Amazon Domination and Gaming the System

Over the past few years, Amazon has grown to become the go-to place for almost everyone looking to buy something online. Thousands of people armed with credit cards lurk the website on a daily basis. Ever since Amazon opened up its platform to third-party sellers, people who were lured by the enormous revenue opportunity and the ease of running an Amazon business began piling up.

Over time, the platform became saturated with sellers peddling all kinds of stuff and some of them even ventured into the weird end of the spectrum. Go on Amazon right now and we bet you can find the following: pizza scissors, (lots and lots of) diapers, bacon-flavored floss, and Nicolas cage rainbow pillow (don't ask, just search).

The competition has gotten so intense that it has become very difficult to capture buyers' attention, especially towards new products.

Then a lightbulb moment came into some sellers' minds: Amazon's rankings are governed by an algorithm, so why not tinker around with the algorithm? Why not game the system? Amazon forbids it, but would they really notice? Would they even care?

Imagine you have a new product that's getting nothing but crickets on Amazon. You know how important reviews are to the ranking algorithm, and you know that you can pay someone to get those reviews for you. Wouldn't you bite the bullet knowing that it could propel your product listing right to where buyers are looking?

Unsurprisingly, many sellers did. Trying to rank a new product using black-hat techniques, or by gaming the system, is much, much easier compared to ranking it the Amazon-legal way. So review buying, Super URLs (unnatural way to boost rankings), and review sabotaging (paying someone to post negative reviews of a competitor's product) has become rampant. So rampant, that Amazon noticed and sent this email en masse to sellers on February 26th, 2018:

Hello,

We are contacting you because you appear to have violate⸱ the policies of "Misuse of ratings, fee⸱back, or reviews", "Misuse of sales rank", "Misuse of Search an⸱ Browse" on our site... If this con⸱uct continues, you will not be eligible to sell on Amazon.com.

Sincerely,
Seller Performance Team

Sellers who received the email were in a state of panic. Most of these sellers have thousands to millions of inventory and revenue tied up on Amazon and being forbidden to sell is the equivalent of an abrupt business death.

Because of how rampant black-hat practices have become, many of these sellers did not even know they were doing something wrong. They wished that someone in Amazon just hit the wrong button and that the whole thing was a mistake.

Mistake or not, it was one of those things that changed our outlook forever on how we do business on Amazon.

It's one of the reasons our Amazon Launch Strategy, and therefore this book, was born.

Part 1

Creating a Plan

Overview of the Launch Strategy

Amazon is the 'place to be' for any ecommerce business. Your brand and its products need to have a presence on this platform, regardless of what stage you're at in your ecommerce journey.

These days building a presence on this massive marketplace is easier said than done. As mentioned before, Amazon has become relevant to the point where it is marked as a target for scheming individuals and organizations who prey on third-party sellers who make an honest living here.

Plan to be different

If you're still planning to get into Amazon, don't let this scare you. Just like the first line says, Amazon is still where you want to be selling (or one of the marketplaces you should be selling in). The key to fighting copycats and product hijackers is to make your brand identity and the products you're selling as unique as possible.

This is where a launch strategy comes in handy. When done right, it can propel an ecommerce business forward, boosting brand popularity, and consequently raising sales for its various products.

Start on the right foot

The right launch strategy can also help owners of ecommerce businesses avoid potential pitfalls. Amazon often uses a heavy hand in dealing with violations. Many who sell their products in this marketplace have received notices, which led to having their seller accounts closed and their product sales frozen. In this regard, setting up your account and listing your products, in a manner that's compliant with the platform's terms and conditions, is crucial.

When you're new to selling on Amazon's platform, executing a proper product launch can be daunting. So we took one of our most popular courses and made it more accessible. In this book, existing concepts have been expanded to offer a deeper look at the specific steps that make up the actual launch process.

Here's what you can expect to learn from this course:

- How to do things that are 100 percent compliant with Amazon's Terms of Service
- Validate products and make sure they are going to react positively on Amazon and potentially in other marketplaces
- Build a list so you can market to people in a 'white hat' way
- White hat tactics to employ to avoid being the recipient of a violation email from Amazon
- Find a product on an online retail service like AliExpress that's similar to the product that you want to develop and launch
- Building the perfect listing for that launch

But before you start developing new products, it's important to test your ideas first. The way to do this is to buy lookalike products then get them in the hands of potential customers. You'll find that several pages of this book talk about the techniques that you can use to do this and do it successfully. Testing with an almost identical yet cheaper version of the product you intend to sell with your target consumers will give you insights on how to make your own products better and more saleable.

How to Short List Products

In the previous chapter, we touched a bit on product development. Part of this endeavor is to be able to glean crucial data from your target audience. The feedback they provide forms the basis for how you will create or develop your own products.

One important aspect of this endeavor is gleaning information from your target audience. In order to do that, you need to send out a similar product into their hands.

Before we go through the process of actually launching a product on Amazon, we first need to go over a very important component of the launch process--the products being launched.

There are a myriad of products out there that you can sell, and while we don't give outright suggestions into what you should sell, here are some useful tips when shortlisting possible products:

Pick a niche

Focusing on a niche will save you time, money, and effort should you decide to expand your product catalog. You wouldn't need to build another list to remarket new products to and you could just essentially reuse your product launch process.

Differentiate in some way

Almost everything you could imagine is sold on the internet today. Strict private labeling no longer works, so make sure that you do something different that will make your products stand out from the competition.

Make sure it's profitable

This one seems like a no-brainer but bear in mind that there might be other costs that you haven't thought about. Factor in shipping, inspection and FBA fees and other costs when calculating profitability.

Do some preliminary research

Get quotes from more than 1 manufacturer. Find out if their MOQ (minimum order quantity) is within your budget and if they allow modification.

Your products are the cornerstone of your launch process and it is paramount that you get your products right if you want the entire process to succeed.

Where and How to Find Lookalike Products

Will this product sell?

You want your Amazon launch to be a success. You want your products to be profitable. However, launching a new product on an untested market is a huge risk.

Designing a sample product, especially when you're not sure how it will be received, is also something we don't recommend. The process alone would have you chipping away at your business capital, even before you've actually had the chance to do a proper product launch.

Opt for a lookalike product

What you should focus on instead is getting a similar product in the hands of would-be customers. You can create a free giveaway around this lookalike product to encourage people to get their hands on it.

The goal of finding a lookalike product is not necessarily to make money, but to validate if the product you intend to launch will resonate with your audience.

Finding the product

Below are the steps necessary to get this done.

Step 1:
Find a product that closely matches the product that you want to develop.

Products can be sourced from online retailers both here and abroad. AliExpress is a good website if you're looking for similar products. Majority of the items sold on this platform are inexpensive. AliExpress also ships for free to the United States. they ship for free to the United States. AliExpress will also be able to do fulfillment for your contest giveaways.

The product you buy does not have to be an exact duplicate. What matters is that it has a high level of similarity.

Step 2:
Purchase more than one sample.

Order the same product from different competitors so you won't have to wait too long for all of them to arrive. Once they do, pick the best one and give it to your photographer for promotional photos and videos that can be used in the giveaway. The images will also be used for reference during the product development stage.

You now know how to find a lookalike product, the next step is to plan the giveaway so you can get that product out there and gauge how well it does in your target market.

Part 2

Validating Your Product

How to Set Up the ClickFunnels Pages

Validating your product is a key step in a successful Amazon product launch. We don't want you to spend thousands of dollars in inventory for a product that no one is going to buy.

In the previous chapter you learned how to find a product that closely resembles what you want to sell. To review, there are two reasons for finding a lookalike product:

1. You want to know if your type of product is something people will buy, without having to commit to a big order.
2. The people who buy will essentially be your beta testers. You can use their feedback and possible complaints to your advantage by modifying your final product and perfecting it even before you launch it on Amazon.

Setting up the Contest Landing Page and Thank You Page

Contests are the starting point of your Amazon launch process. It is a two-pronged approach: it allows you to capture leads and build an email list (very important) while validating your product idea.

We set up contests and giveaways using ClickFunnels and the following lessons assume that you already have a ClickFunnels account. If you don't you can use our affiliate link (**www.ecomcrew.com/clickfunnels**) to sign up for one.

We've also made it easy for you by providing you with a ClickFunnels template that you can simply clone and plug your details in.

To set up your Contest and Thank You landing pages, do the following:

1. Go to **https://www.ecomcrew.com/optinfunnel** to clone the free Optin Funnel template.
2. This is how the cloned funnel looks like. Click on **Settings** to begin customizing it.

3. Change the Name, Path, Domain, SMTP Configuration, and Favicon URL. You can also add the Facebook Pixel and Google Analytics in the Head Tracking Code.

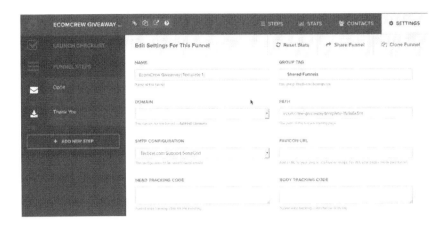

4. Go back to the **Optin** page and click **Edit Page**.

5. Customize the page with your branding. Use the promotional photos and videos you've taken of the sample lookalike product you ordered from the last chapter.

6. Customize the popup that will show up when the CTA is clicked. From the page editor, mouse over **Pop Up** and click **Show Pop Up**. Clicking on the fields will show a sidebar where you can edit the pop up details.

Integrating ClickFunnels with UpViral

You will need to create your giveaway using a platform like Gleam (https://gleam.io/) or Upviral (https://upviral.com/). We used Upviral for our contest and below is how we integrated it with our ClickFunnels pages:

1. Under **Settings** from the Page Editor of Upviral, click **Integrations**. This is where you'll integrate ClickFunnels with UpViral.

Tip: When creating a giveaway on UpViral, make an effort to make your Share Widget look good (ours even include a video).

2. Once you're done creating your giveaway, click **Installation** under **Review Campaign**. You'll be sent to the page below which gives you a series of integration steps to follow:

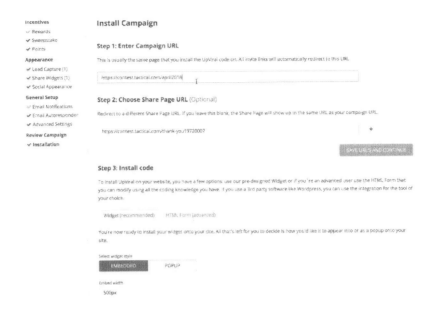

3. Enter your Optin page URL in the **Campaign URL box** (Step 1), and your Thank You page URL in the **Share Page UR**L (Step 2).

4. In Step 3, click on **HTML Form (advanced)** and you'll find 3 sets of code you'll need to copy and paste into 3 locations in your ClickFunnels page:

    a. In the <body> tag of your lead capture page (copy the code). In your contest funnel, go to **Optin page** > **Edit Page** > **Settings** > **Integrations** and you'll see the form on the next image:

Input these values:

Integration = UpViral Form (Html Form)

Action = Integate Existing Form (Add HTML Below)

Paste Web Form Code (HTML) = the code you just

copied from UpViral

Click **Parse and Save Web Form**.

Scroll down, then match up the name and email from the values in the drop down.

b. In the header or footer or your lead capture page (copy the code).

Go to **Optin > Edit Page > Settings > Tracking code**.

Paste the code you just copied.

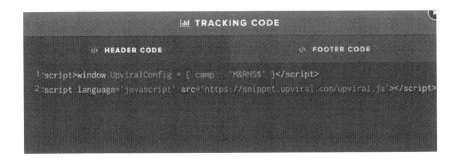

c. Where you want your share widget to appear (copy the code).

Go to your **Thank You page** > **Edit Page**.

Click on **Custom JavaScript/HTML** then **Open Code Editor** and paste the code you just copied in the text box that appears.

5. In your Thank You page, go to **Edit Page** > **Settings** > **Tracking Code**, and make sure you have the following code:

Setting up your email list and email sequence

Your email list is as essential to your launch as your lookalike product itself. You need to be able to capture the email of every person who enters your contest. This is how you do it:

1. Create an email list in Actionetics for giveaway entrants.
2. Go back to your contest funnel, click **Optin** > **Automation**, then click **Add New Action**. Choose Everyone under **Condition**, Add to List under **Action To Do,** and then select the email list you just created under **With...**

3. Set up your email sequence by going to **Actionetics** > **Action Funnels** > **New Action Funnel**. Create an email flow like the

one below (you can find swipe files for these emails in the Resources page of this book):

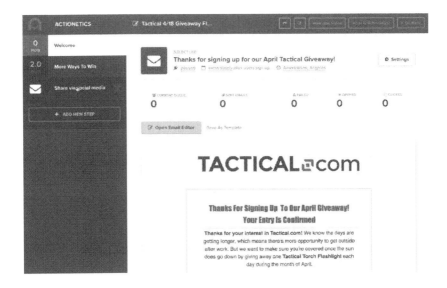

That's it! You just set up your own contests page plus your email list. Don't forget to test it out!

Setting Up Your Product Sales Page in ClickFunnels

You already picked and ordered your lookalike product, set your contest pages up, and set up your email list. You now have all the ingredients for your product validation phase.

Let's get started with the fun bit.

Start running your giveaway by promoting it on social media. The Share Widget that you configured on Upviral will give participants the ability to share the giveaway in exchange for more entries. Let social media do its magic. You'll have thousands of email sign ups this way if you run your giveaway long enough.

The duration of the giveaway and the number of prizes you give out will depend on the number of emails you want to gather and the value of your prize. For example, you could potentially give a prize daily for a product that's $10 below. For more expensive items, you could give away one product per week or twice per month. We found that the giveaway is most effective if there are daily winners, though.

You also need to set a goal of how many subscribers you want in your email list. Once you've hit that number, you can stop the giveaway and proceed to the product validation phase.

Setting Up Your Product Sales Page

Let's assume that the product you picked as a prize costs $5 and you intend to give one out daily in your giveaway. Your goal is to get 5,000 people in your email list. Let's say you hit that goal within a month, so you have 5,000 emails and 30 winners. Sure, you're going to send notification emails to those who got picked. But what do you do with the 4,970 who didn't win?

These 4,970 people who didn't win the contest are the most important part of your product validation phase.

The idea here is to see whether or not these people who expressed interest in your prize will be willing to buy the same thing at a "heavily discounted price". Our price point at this stage is usually just to break-even (we'll be selling the final product for a lot more later on). Our goal at this point is not to make money but to validate the product idea.

A product sales page allows you to verify if the people on the list you've compiled will actually buy your product. By providing data on important statistics like conversion rate, you get an idea of how well the product you're developing will sell on Amazon and eventually on your own online store.

Setting up a product sales page should be done after the contest you initiated is over. By this time, you should have built a list of potential customers for the product that you expect to launch.
A product sales page in ClickFunnels is made up of four parts.

1. Product landing page
2. Sales page
3. Order form
4. Thank You page

As in the previous lesson, we've made the process of setting up ClickFunnels pages much easier for you by creating a customizable template.

To access this template, go to this link while you're logged into your ClickFunnels account: **https://www.ecomcrew.com/salesfunnel**

1. You should find yourself in the *Sales Page*. Click on the **EDIT** button to customize this section.

2. Add a product image and create your offer. Again, you can use the images you've taken of the lookalike product you ordered earlier.

3. Customize the **CALL TO ACTION** button by changing the text and color.

4. Adjust the settings for the countdown timer on your offer. We usually let our offers run for 5 days but you can use any other time duration you want.

5. Give people more information about the product you're selling. Identify three key functions of the product in the *Feature Hea•line* section. You can go into detail on these in the *Feature or Benefit Hea•line.*

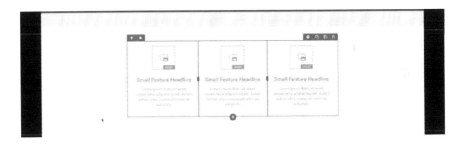

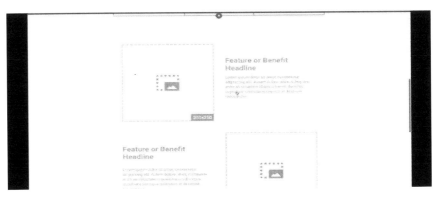

6. Customize the countdown timer on the bottom of the page as well as the footer.

7. You're done with the **Sales Page** at this point. Before moving to the next section of the funnel (**Order Form**), you'll need to add your product first.

8. Once the window on the next image pops up, fill out the boxes with all the necessary information about your product.

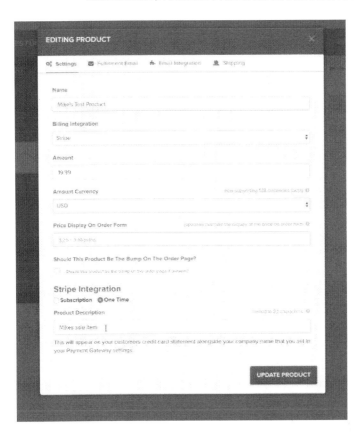

9. Tab over to **Fulfillment Email** and customize the body text as

   needed. You may want to replace the text that

   says #PRODUCT_THANK_YOU_PAGE# with the appropriate
   link or just remove it. Hit **UPDATE PRODUCT** when you're

   done.

10. Proceed to **Email Integration** and customize as needed. Select your integration method and fill out the other boxes as needed.

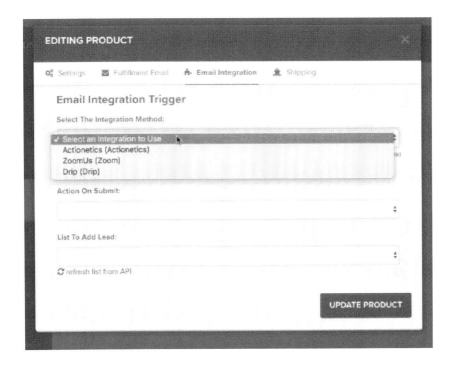

11. Now that you have your product on there, it's time to create the **Order Form**.

12. Fill this out the necessary details and add a product image.

13. After coming up with your product's order form, you have the option to upsell products. To to this, click again on the **PRODUCTS** button.

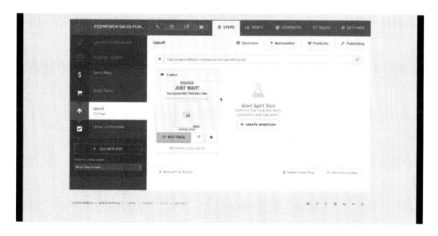

14. On the Add New Product window, create a listing for your upsell product. It could be the same product you are selling but at a discounted price, as shown in the screenshot on the next image.

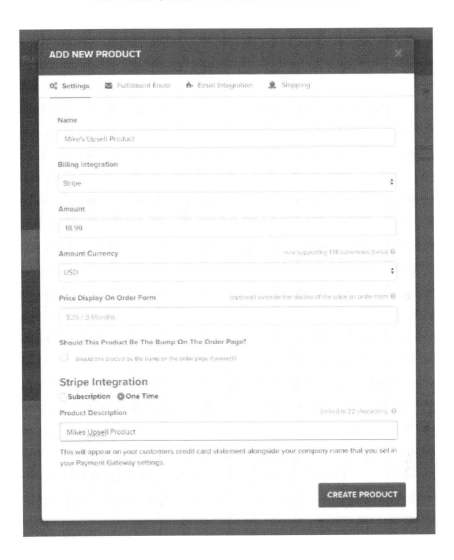

15. Now that you're done creating the listing for the product you want to upsell, you can proceed to creating an offer for it. Clicking on the **Upsell** section of the funnel will open up a page where you can customize your upsell offer. Just add the text, image, and edit the call to action button at the bottom of the page.

16. Finally, you've reached the **Order Confirmation** section of the funnel. As with the previous sections, customize this page as necessary. Add your company logo, social media channels, and website domain at the bottom.

Setting Up Your Facebook Ads

Social word of mouth is a great way to get eyeballs on your giveaway (that's why we want our Share Widget to look good), but relying on organic shares alone is not enough to reach your goal in a short time.

This is where Facebook ads come in. Facebook is a great way to connect and interact with people by demographic, making targeting a lot more effective.

For us, advertising on Facebook is a no-brainer. In this section, we'd like to share with you how we run Facebook ads and some best practices to keep in mind.

Methodology

There are two ways by which you can spread the word about a contest on Facebook:

1. Create a post about the contest that you can pin at the top of your wall for visibility during the contest period. This will then be boosted to reach different groups of people.
2. Create a Facebook ad with a headline and a button that redirects to the actual contest page.

To better visualize these, see the screenshot below.

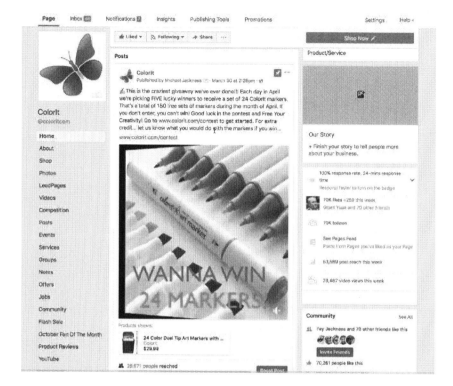

On testing these two methodologies, we found the first one to be effective because it was more prominent on our page and therefore easier to recall.

Creating a Contest or Giveaway Post

Here are some tips on how to create an eye-catching contest post on Facebook.

1. Make sure your post contains all the information about the giveaway.
2. Include a link to the actual contest or giveaway page.

3. Use emoticons to draw the attention of readers.

Boosting a Contest or Giveaway Post

Below are some best practices for boosting a post:

1. If you have more than 500 fans a day, boost to them first for at least a day.
2. Boost to core group. Those that fit your customer demographic and have most likely bought a product or two from you in the past.
3. Keep ad spend at below $0.60 per lead.
4. Make sure your product aligns with groups on Facebook that have an interest that fits your product

Setting Up Your Email Funnel

Running a contest doesn't just test the waters for the product you intend to develop. It is also a great way to build an email list of prospective customers for your brand. One of the ultimate goals of this launch strategy is to get more people to sign up to your email list as cheaply as possible.

ClickFunnels is great for tool to use in our launch strategy because of its email integration. The more people that sign up to your mailing list, the cheaper it will be to advertise to those who are already a part of the list.

But what if you already have a list? What then do you do with all those email addresses? You target them for your email marketing.

In this lesson, we'll show you how to setup your email funnel.

Learning the jargon

When setting up your email funnel, it's important to be familiar with its makeup.

There are two parts:

List. This refers to the bucket that holds all those email addresses and other contact information derived from the customer.

Action Funnel. This is your actual email sequence. It is composed of a number of emails aimed at enabling the recipient to convert (e.g., purchase the product).

Let's have a look at what an action funnel looks like.

1. In the example below, we have a sequence that's composed of three emails. This sequence is intended to take the recipient through the giveaway cycle. The first email is what's called a welcome email.

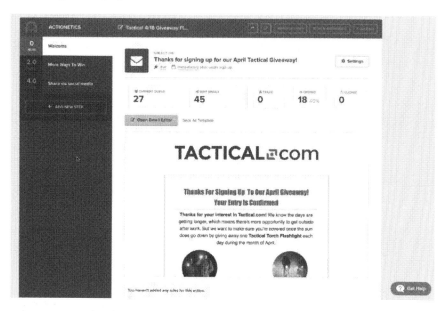

2. Email number two on the sequence encourages the recipient to submit more entries to increase the chances to win the featured giveaway.

3. Making a bid to increase your social media followers can also be built into your email sequence. In this third email, we are actively promoting our different social media channels.

When the contest period is over and the winners have been drawn, you can then launch another email sequence that will be sent to the non-winners. Our two-email sequence looks something like this.

1. The first email serves to notify the non-winning recipient. It also provides an option for those who want to buy the product that served as the giveaway prize.

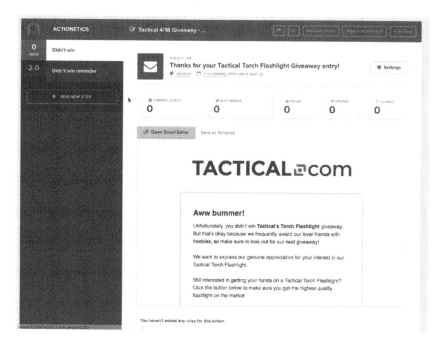

2. The second email is a reminder, with information on how people can purchase the product.

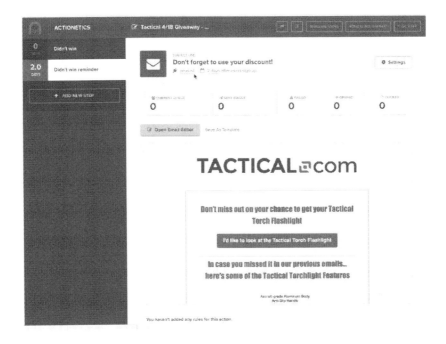

In the next couple of lessons, we'll be showing you how to create emails for both the winners and the non-winners.

Setting Up Your Winners Email

You've just learned how to set up a product sales page funnel and run it together with your promotional giveaway. When the contest is over, the next order of business is to notify the winners via email.

We use an email management tool called Help Scout to send out emails to those on our subscriber list. You may also use Upviral to do this or even Gmail.

The way we do it is to send two separate emails, which we'll discuss in detail below.

Notification Email

As the label implies, the notification email is sent to winners. Essentially, it contains the instructions for how they can claim their prize. See the screenshot on the next page for an example.

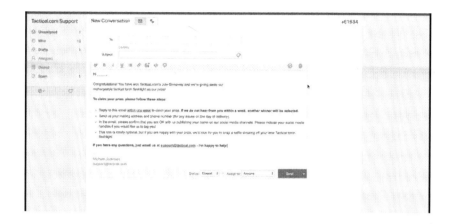

Confirmation Email

Once you hear back from the winner, you can then send a confirmation email detailing when that person can expect to receive the prize in the email. Don't forget to show your appreciation that they took part in the giveaway and patronized your products.

Setting Up Your Non-Winners Email

So you got 5,000 people to sign up for your contest. Great! Assuming you ran the giveaway for a month with one winner each day, you have 30 winners you just sent a notification email to.

So what do you do with the 4,970 people who didn't win?

Reaching out to non-winners is more important than emailing the winners. This is because these people will become the core of your product validation phase. They expressed interest in your product during the contest page, and now we'll try to find out if they will be interested in actually buying the product at a discount.

The idea is to test and see if they will buy this product that you had as a giveaway. You should aim for at least 15% open rate, preferably getting to the 20 percent range. If you reach or exceed this, then you know you have a winner.

Setting up your email

Now let's get on to the specific steps for setting this up in ClickFunnels.

1. Creating an email sequence for non-winners can take as little as two emails. The first one should: a) break the bad news b) provide an opportunity to purchase the giveaway product.

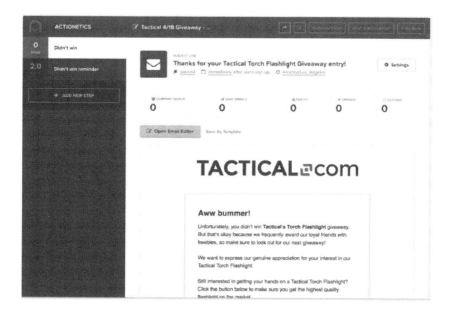

You can find a template for this email by going to **https://www.ecomcrew.com/swipefilesdoc** for the Word document or **https://www.ecomcrew.com/swipefilespdf** for the PDF version.

On the bottom part of the email, you'll find that there's a call to action button that leads to the actual product page.

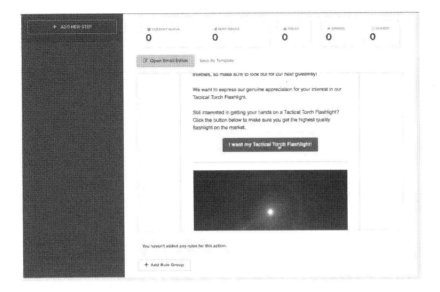

The product page should include high-quality images of the product in various angles as well as descriptions of the features and uses that it has.

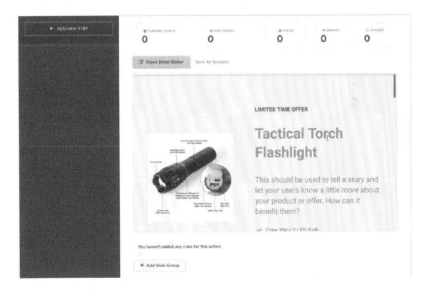

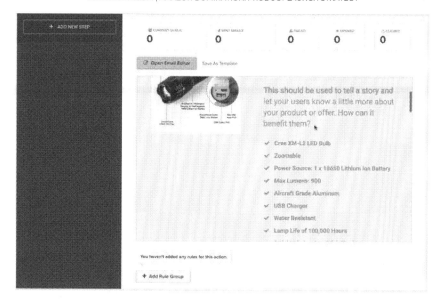

Normally, you'll have the product available at a discounted price. To reinforce a sense of urgency, a countdown timer at the bottom of the page is a good addition.

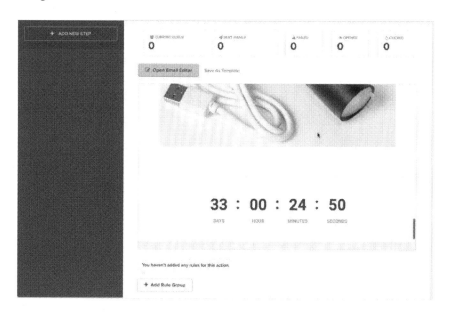

2. The second email will serve as a reminder to purchase the giveaway product within the "limited offer" period.

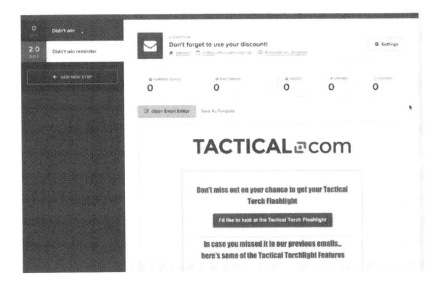

The number of emails will depend on your particular audience. We've gotten away with three emails for some brands, but to be on the safe side, two should do the trick.

Setting Up Amazon Coupon Emails

A big chunk of our company's profit comes from email marketing. Our Shopify stores get 50% of sales from this very source. As you can probably tell, it's a strategy that's near and dear to our hearts.

Email sequences can do more than help run and set up your giveaway campaigns. You can also resurrect listings and give life to new products quickly by sending out what we call Amazon Coupon Emails.

Amazon Coupon Emails: what are they?

Amazon Coupon Emails are a series of emails containing a a coupon code people can use for specific products on Amazon. People are first directed into a landing page that collects their email in exchange for a coupon code. Once they opt in, you send them a series of emails that contain the coupon code.

A little bit of warning...

While very useful, we only use Amazon coupon emails sparingly. Specifically, we only use them when one of these two things happen:

1. We have a listing that has been languishing lately and we want to send some traffic to it
2. A product launch is not as successful as we want it to be, and as a last resort, we send new traffic to the product listing using coupons

Amazon coupon emails drive astonishing traffic to your listing when your discount is attractive enough. So why do we use such a powerful tool very sparingly?

The reason for this lies in how Amazon's algorithm works. If a listing experiences a sudden surge of traffic in one day, and most conversions from this traffic are associated with a coupon, it could trigger Amazon to flag your listing, as this would seem unnatural.

In relation to this, we never use coupons to give a very deep discount. Anything that's bought with a 40% or higher discount will have unverified reviews. The effect gets compounded and is a lot worse in Amazon's eyes if these conversions with very deep discounts came from a sudden surge in traffic. *We want to avoi⦁ suspicion from Amazon as much as possible, so try to use Amazon Coupon Emails only when absolutely necessary.*

Now that that's out of the way, let's get into the actual steps.

How to set it up

We've made it easier for you to set up your Amazon Coupon Emails. Just go to **https://www.ecomcrew.com/amazonoptinfunnel** to copy the funnel template.

1. In the template we created within ClickFunnels, there should be two sections - *Optin* and *Thank You.*

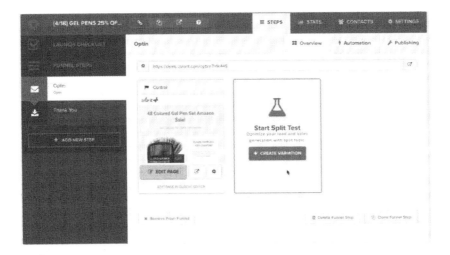

2. The *Optin* section contains detailed product information about the item that you're selling at a discounted price. In this example, it's the ColorIt 48 Colored Gel Pen Set. Note that this product page is customizable. You can drag and drop elements that will suit your brand. A countdown timer is added at the very end to establish a sense of urgency.

Variety of Uses

Use these coloring gel pens for a variety of projects. Whether it be creating a shopping list, doodling, scrapbooking, coloring, or creating decorations you'll be able to add a pop of color everywhere you go!

Gel Pen Case & Refills for Endless Creativity

Use the convenient coloring gel pen case to take your creativity on the go. We also include an extra pack of refills in every order, so you don't have to worry about running out!

08 : 01 : 52 : 51
DAYS · HOUR · MINUTES · SECONDS

3. Clicking on the blue **SEND ME THE COUPON** button takes the user to the *Thank You* section. This page contains detailed instructions for getting the discount.

4. If you're using Actionetics in conjunction with ClickFunnels, you'll need to set up this promo properly. The first thing you need to do is add your list. Go to **Settings** and select **Email Integrations**.

5. Proceed by adding the appropriate list as show in the screenshot below.

6. Next, you'll need to set up an action funnel for this specific promo. Go back to the main funnel and direct your cursor to the **Actionetics** tab on the top navigation. From the options, select **Action Funnels**.

7. For our ColorIt 48 Colored Gel Pen Set, we've created an email sequence composed of two emails. The first email contains details about the promo and, most importantly, the coupon code customers can use to get 25% off on their purchase.

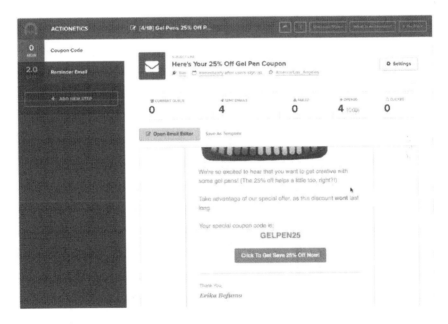

8. The second email in the sequence is a reminder to purchase our gel pen set within the time period specified to be able to enjoy the discount.

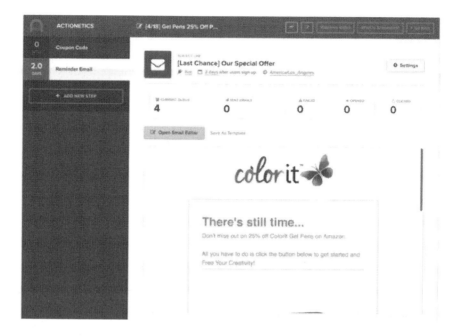

9. Finally, don't forget to add your lead pixel to your *Thank You* page. This is especially important if you're running Facebook ads to your landing page. Make sure to plop the CSS script on the Tracking Code.

    You can get to the Tracking Code by clicking **Settings** and then selecting **Tracking Code** from the drop down menu. Refer to the screenshots on the next page.

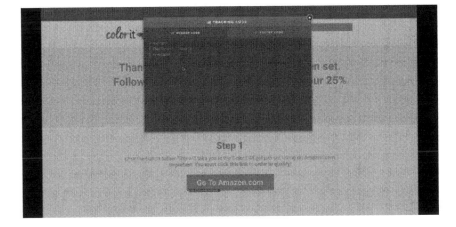

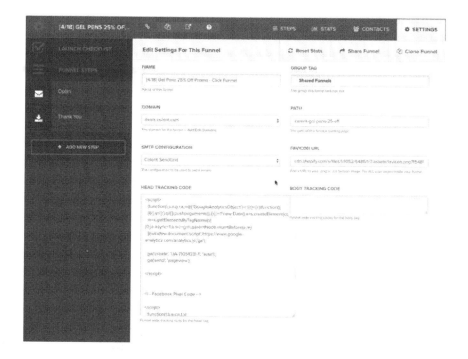

Again, we'd like to emphasize that this bonus funnel is ideally used for items languishing on Amazon.

Remember, the moving average on Amazon is really important. So if you have a $1k to spend on this promotion, it's best to space out your spending to a couple of days. For example, you can use spend at most $50/day over a three week period.

Part 3

Amazon Product Launch

Amazon Optimization - The Importance of Product Photography

Now that you've created a plan and validated your product, it's time to prepare for the main event--your product launch.

Since your listing will be the at center of your product launch, you need to be certain that everything in your listing is perfect. All your efforts planning and validating your product will be wasted if you won't be able to sell anything, all because of a bad listing.

Never skimp on product photography

One of the biggest mistakes sellers make is skimping on photography. You must NEVER, EVER do this. Your product photos are the key to your buyers' imagination and is the biggest factor in getting them to buy something they can't physically hold.

By "not skimping on photography" we not only mean getting high-quality photos of your product in a white background. We also mean getting lifestyle shots with your product actually being used, and infographics that showcase the special attributes/features of your product.

As part of this book, we provide you with templates you can use for your product photography. You can find them here: **https://www.ecomcrew.com/photography-light** and **https://www.ecomcrew.com/photography-dark**.

Why it's a big deal

If you think that getting good product photography is way too much effort or if you think that it's not that important anyway, check out the actual stats of some of our products for which we recently optimized with good product photos:

Before optimization:

After optimization:

You can see that our conversion rate increased from 9.7% to 23.0% after we optimized our product photos. What's even more amazing is that the increase happened during our off-season.

Good product photography can also affect one other thing indirectly: rankings.

In the graph below, you can see on the lower left-hand side that we used to rank on the 10th page or lower for our target keywords. Looking at the right though, you can see that rankings improved significantly after we optimized our product photos. Apart from a few outliers, we now rank higher, with many of our products appearing on the first page.

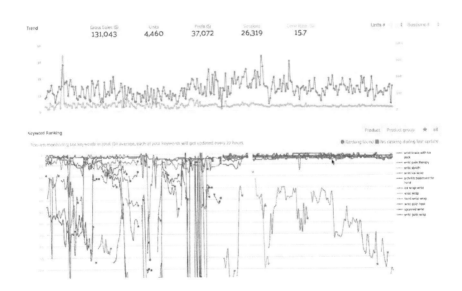

As you can see, it really pays off to go the extra mile and get good product photos.

Amazon Optimization - Product Titles

Arguably the most important part of your listing is your product title. Almost on par with photography, product titles are indisputably critical to your listing performance.

In this lesson we will teach how to create optimized product titles that will boost your clickthrough rate and improve keywords search rankings.

Parts of a good product title

In order to illustrate how to come up with optimized titles, take a look at the listing on the next page:

This is an example of a listing that has an optimized title. As you can see on the next image, it appears on the first page of the search results of a keyword we're optimizing for: **wrist ice pack**.

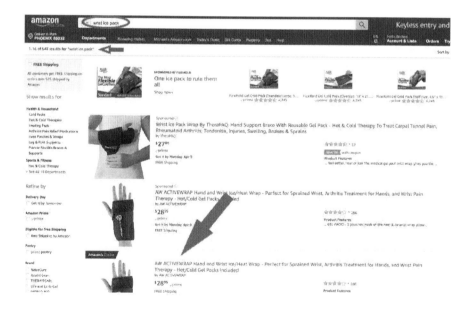

Now let's break the product title down and examine each part.

AW ACTIVEWRAP Hand and Wrist Ice/Heat Wrap - Perfect for Sprained Wrist, Arthritis Treatment for Hands, and Wrist Pain Therapy - Hot/Cold Gel Packs Included

- **AW ACTIVEWRAP** - This is your product trademark. There are two reasons why we put this in the beginning: Amazon seems to be in the process of requiring this, and it helps with brand awareness.
- **Hand and Wrist Ice/Heat Wrap** - This is the name of your product or a description of what it is.
- **Perfect for Sprained Wrist, Arthritis Treatment for Hands, and Wrist Pain Therapy** - This part describes what the product is for and attracts buyers to click on your listing.
- **Hot/Cold Gel Packs Included** - This is an answer to the most common question we get asked about this particular product. Putting it here eliminates an uncertainty in a buyer's mind before they even click on the listing. Alternatively, you can describe a unique proposition your product has in this part.

Best practices

Here are some things to keep in mind when creating a good product title:

1. Don't overstuff your title with keywords.
2. Make it short and concise enough to give buyers a clear idea of what your product is.
3. Always, always split test.

The main idea here is to optimize your product titles in a way that makes it easier for potential buyers to make positive decisions about your product.

Don't attempt to write something you think appeals to Amazon's ranking algorithm but gives buyers a negative experience. Remember, Amazon's algorithm is always changing to ultimately make everything easier for buyers. With that in mind, always create titles intended for people, not for Amazon's bots.

Amazon Optimization - Bullet Points and Descriptions

Now that you've optimized your product photography and title, it's time to shift our focus on optimizing the rest of your listing.

In this lesson we'll optimize bullet points, Enhanced Brand Content, and description.

Bullet Points

While arguably the majority of online shoppers look only at the title and photos, a huge number of people read bullet points before making a buying decision. Your goal here is to answer whatever possible question or doubt they might have in mind, while showcasing what makes your product better than everybody else's.

DO's:
- Don't write very long bullet points. The shorter the better.
- Highlight very important words in bold. These words could describe features/unique proposition of your product.
- Include answers to frequently asked questions, but limit this to the most important ones.

DON'Ts:

- DO NOT use the green checkmark black hat.
- Don't stuff your bullet points with keywords.

Below is an example of a listing with good bullet points:

Colorlt

Colorlt Gel Pens For Adult Coloring Books – Premium Ink Gel Pens Set With Case Includes 48 Artist Quality Coloring Pens: 24 Glitter, 12 Metallic, 12 Neon Plus 48 Matching Refills For 96 Total Pieces

★★★★☆ ▾   872 customer reviews | 51 answered questions

Amazon's Choice for "colorit gel pens"

List Price: ~~$39.99~~
    Price: **$29.99** & **FREE Shipping**. Details
You Save: $10.00 (25%)

Get $10 off instantly: Pay $19.99 upon approval for the Amazon Prime Store Card.

✓prime | Try Fast, Free Shipping ▾

In Stock.
Want it tomorrow, April 7 to 85032? Order within 16 hrs and choose **One-Day Shipping** at checkout.
Sold by Terran LLC and Fulfilled by Amazon. Gift-wrap available.

- HIGH QUALITY AND LONG-LASTING ~ The Colorit Colored Gel Pen set includes 48 long-lasting gel ink pens: glitter gel pens, metallic gel pens, and neon gel pens. The ink is housed in a transparent barrel that is labeled with the color name and color code. Each set also comes with a comfort grip for extended support and 48 coded ink refills.
- NON-TOXIC AND ACID-FREE - The coloring pens are non-toxic, acid-free, and water-based ink, making them safe for anyone to use. Whether this is a gift or you love gel pens, the Colorit Gel Pen set is ideal for everyday use. Great for: writing, journaling, scribbling, doodling, drawing, and of course coloring.
- SMOOTH APPLICATION – The fine 0.8mm - 1.0mm ballpoint tip allows for smooth and precise color application. Bring your artwork to life by using the Colorit Gel Pen set to fill in tiny details and add a little sparkle to your designs. Perfect gel pens for adult coloring books.
- PORTABLE STORAGE CASE AND MAGNETIC GIFT BOX – Take your Colorit Gel Pen Set wherever you go for non-stop creativity. The travel pen case with individual inserts provides a nice option to stay organized, keeping your pens in good condition. For extra art supplies, you can use the Colorit Gift Box as a handy storage option.
- 100% SATISFACTION GUARANTEE — If you are not satisfied or would like to exchange your product, we are happy to do so WITHIN 30 DAYS of your purchase date.

Enhanced Brand Content

Enhanced Brand Content (EBC or A+) is a feature within Amazon that allows you to add special formatting to your product descriptions. Amazon estimates that A+ content can increase conversions by 3-10%. Get brand registered as soon as possible so you can take advantage of this feature early on.

Below is an example of EBC:

Have a question?

Find answers in product info, Q&As, reviews

Replaces 7 Common
Kitchen Appliances in 1

Pressure Cooker, Slow Cooker, Rice

Easy One Touch Controls

Simple as pressing a button.

Consistent Results, 3rd
Generation Technology

Built-in microprocessor monitors

Alexa Skill & Free App

Alexa guided cooking, 500+ Recipes,
Getting Started Videos, Favorite Recipe

Description

Although descriptions no longer seem to be an important ranking factor, you should not disregard them altogether. Write your product features, guarantees, and any other important information.

Tip: Include Spanish keywords in your description for those who search Amazon in Spanish.

Things to keep in mind

You product title and photography are by far the most important parts of your listing and you need to spend a considerable amount of time and effort on them.

However, don't skimp on the little details. Buyers will have more confidence to buy from you when they see that you put effort into even the smallest part of your listing.

Lastly, don't overstuff your listing with keywords in an attempt to rank. Always remember that conversion is the number 1 ranking factor, so write for people and not Amazon bots.

Amazon Optimization - Turn On Sponsored Products

Now that your listing is ready, it's time to turn on Amazon PPC.

Although this lesson is not a deep dive on PPC, what we'll discuss here will be enough to get your campaigns up and running on launch and generate initial sales.

Before we begin...

Before we even start with PPC, we want to clarify that at this point our priority are initial sales and identification of converting keywords. We are NOT focusing on profitability especially at the first week of launching, AND we will be spending a considerable amount of money. Take this into account when budgeting your ad spend.

Now that we have that out of the way, let's proceed to the steps on how to activate and optimize Amazon PPC.

1. Know your keywords

The first step before even turning on PPC is to know what keywords you want to rank for. You need to give Amazon an idea about what your product is, and this is necessary for the next step.

Tip: Don't try to rank for high-traffic but very broad keywords. For example, if you're selling an ice pack for wrists, don't try to rank for the term "ice pack". Try to be more specific, i.e., "wrist ice pack", "cold wrap for wrists", etc.

Make sure your keywords are included in your backend and integrated throughout your listing.

2. Turn on Automatic Campaign

Instead of manually targeting the keywords in step 1, we will let Amazon do its thing using an Automatic Campaign. Amazon will find which search terms actually generate sales based on the keywords you've set up in step 1.

To set an automatic campaign, take a look at the next image:

CAMPAIGN SETTINGS | CREATE AD GROUP

1 | 2

Set your campaign budget and duration

Campaign name

Activewrap Wrist Automatic

Daily budget

$500.00

$1.00 minimum

Start date | **End date**

04/06/2018 | No end date

Select a targeting type

⦿ **Automatic targeting**
Save time and let Amazon target your ads to all relevant customer searches based on your product info. Learn more

○ **Manual targeting**
Your ads appear when a customer's search matches keywords that you provide. Learn more

Cancel | Continue to next step

You might have noticed that we set the daily budget to $500. Keep in mind that profitability is not a priority during launch week so we set the daily budget as high as we can.

When setting an Ad Group, take a look at the next image.

Name this group of ads

Ad group name

Ad Group 1

Only visible when managing your ads

Choose products to advertise

Search by product name ⬍ | 🔍 activewrap wrist | **Search**

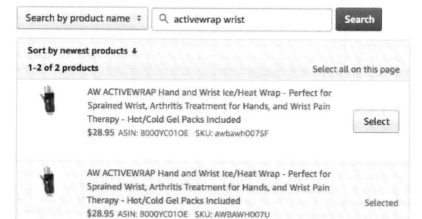

Sort by newest products ⬇

1-2 of 2 products   Select all on this page

AW ACTIVEWRAP Hand and Wrist Ice/Heat Wrap - Perfect for Sprained Wrist, Arthritis Treatment for Hands, and Wrist Pain Therapy - Hot/Cold Gel Packs Included
$28.95 ASIN: B000YC01OE   SKU: awbawh007SF   **Select**

AW ACTIVEWRAP Hand and Wrist Ice/Heat Wrap - Perfect for Sprained Wrist, Arthritis Treatment for Hands, and Wrist Pain Therapy - Hot/Cold Gel Packs Included
$28.95 ASIN: B000YC01OE   SKU: AWBAWH007U   Selected

⟵ Previous | 1 | Next ⟶

1 products selected

AW ACTIVEWRAP Hand and Wrist Ice/Heat Wrap - Perfect for Sprained Wrist, Arthritis Treatment for Hands, and Wrist Pain Therapy - Hot/Cold Gel Packs Included   ✕
$28.95   ASIN: B000YC01OE   SKU: AWBAWH007U

Default bid

1.64

Suggested bid: $1.30   Bid range: $0.38 - $2.25

Back | Save and finish

We try to bid 25% higher than the median bid, and that works out to be $1.64.

Tip: To make things easier, set up an account with Sellics (**http://www.ecomcrew.com/sellics** - affiliate link) and let it do the automatic bidding for you.

3. Turn on Manual Campaigns

After your Automatic campaign has been running for a month, check Sellics and look for keywords that generate the most sales.

Take these keywords and create manual campaigns for them. Make a Manual Campaign Exact and Manual Campaign Phrase for these keywords. Finally, add the exact phrases as negative exact in the Automatic Campaign and Manual Campaign Phrase.

4. "Massage" your listing

Finally, optimize your listing again to include the keywords you just extracted from step 3. Put them in your description and bullet points. If there is a keyword that converts exceptionally well, include it in your title.

In the next lesson we will look at Amazon Headline Search Ads.

Amazon Optimization - Turn On Amazon Headline Search Ads

Headline search ads get a lot of exposure because they are displayed before any search results, right below the search bar.

This alone is enough reason for you to capitalize on headline search ads, but because of Amazon's requirements, there are not a lot of people who can take advantage of this. Some don't even know how to use it.

Requirements

In order to use headline search ads, you need to be brand registered AND have at least 3 related products.

The more challenging requirement here is having at least 3 related products that can rank for the same set of keywords. If you're still in the development phase, you could try to make 3 variations (colors, sizes, etc.). There are products that are really difficult or expensive to make 3 variations of though, so if you don't have them now, you can just skip on this lesson and come back later.

But if you have 3 related products and your brand is already brand registered, here are the steps on how to create headline search ads:

1. Choose where to drive your ad traffic

We usually choose Product list page, as you can see in the next image. You can also see the requirement to add 3 products or more:

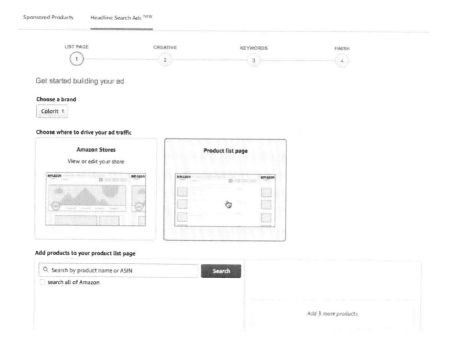

Here's how a product list page will actually look like:

2. Add your headline and review

Enter your headline copy and look at the preview of how it will be displayed. Tip: Don't write long headlines as it can shrink your text size.

3. Set your bid and keywords

Set your bid and keywords as you can see on the next image. Add the keywords you generated in the previous lesson in this step. You can keep on updating this as you get more targeted keywords from your Automatic Campaign.

In the next lesson we'll finally talk about launching to your email list.

Amazon Optimization - Emailing Your List in Segments

You've optimized your listing. You've run PPC and headline search ads. Your inventory is already sitting in FBA warehouses.

You've finally come to the big day--launch day.

Remember the list of emails you've accumulated during the giveaway phase? It's time to make use of that. We will now let everyone on that list know that your product is finally up on Amazon.

But first let's divide your list into segments.

Why should you email your list in segments?

We are dripping our email campaign and not do it all in one go because we want to show Amazon consistent and sustainable sales over a certain period of time. You'll have a better standing in the eyes of Amazon if you sell 100 items in a day in the course of 10 days than to have a thousand sales in one day and zero the next following days.

We divide your list into 5 segments and send a launch email to one segment per day. You can then circle back to the first list on the 6th day until you reach the 10th day.

Sending your email blast

If you're using Actionetics, you can download your entire list in a CSV format and manually divide it into 5. You can then reupload the 5 lists back into Actionetics. You don't need to do this if you're using a different email client as they have a built-in way to divide your list into segments.

Create your email broadcast in Actionetics and fill out the fields on the next image:

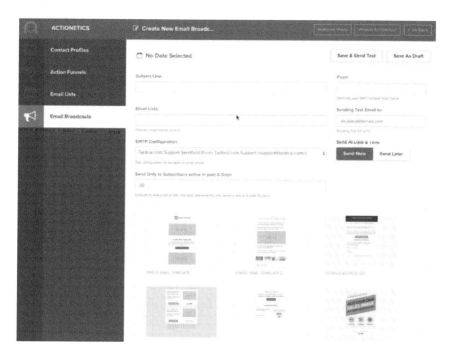

Don't forget to use an affiliate link when you send people to your Amazon listing so you can track your conversion rate.

Ideally your conversion rate should double or triple the conversion rate during your validation phase. If you don't see desirable results, you can offer coupons when you circle back to your first list on the 6th day.

Bonus - Launching to Your Facebook Audience

One of the things that we emphasize in this course is the importance of getting outside traffic to Amazon. One of the ways to get outside traffic is by directing your Facebook audience to Amazon via Facebook ads.

Outside traffic, not profitability

Just like with PPC, our priority over the next few days is not profitability. At this point we want to build traction on sales and outside traffic to Amazon, which is very important.

Keep in this in mind when setting your ad budget.

How to and best practices

- Post an announcement that your product is already live on Amazon and boost it to your audience using data from your giveaway phase.
- Try using a video if you can. Videos convert better than images.
- Don't use an affiliate link when sending people to Amazon from Facebook. This is against Amazon TOS.

- Set a budget of at least $10 per day. The higher the better.

Make use of the data that you've gathered during your giveaway phase and tweak your process according to ad performance. Don't focus on profitability at this point--getting just one or two sales can already make a big difference.

Bonus - Launching to Influencers

Your launch week constitutes of well orchestrated and synchronized activities, most of which were covered in the previous lessons.

We've finally come to the last piece of the puzzle--launching to influencers.

What are influencers?

Influencers are people with blogs and social media accounts who have a substantial following in a particular niche. They can create blog posts, unboxings, review videos, and social media posts for brands they collaborate with.

They can get a lot of eyeballs in front of your product and are ideal for brand awareness and off-Amazon traffic.

How to make use of influencers

There are two ways to reach out to influencers you'd like to work with.

You can search for people who have good following in the niche you're operating in. You can manually reach out to them with offers of free products, free prizes for their giveaways, or you can offer to pay them with cash.

An easier way to find influencers would be to use Famebit. People who are in this platform are actively looking for brands to collaborate with so you have a much higher chance of getting a positive reply.

Best practices

- Find at least 10 influencers.
- Ask your manufacturer to airship 10 products ahead of your main shipment so you can send products to influencers in advance of your launch.
- Let each influencer know about your launch date and ask them not to post their content until you're ready.

- During your launch week, spread out influencer content over the next 10 days, ideally one content per day.
- Let them use their own affiliate link.

Influencers are excellent for brand awareness. While we ideally want one influencer content going live per day, a lot of influencers follow a regular posting schedule and you need to respect this. Just make sure that your content is spread out throughout your launch week.

Conclusion

You're all set!

You've made it to the end of this book and we couldn't be more proud. We hope you use this information when taking the next step in your Amazon journey. We're very happy to think that another seller, who is honest and interested only in real business growth and not short-term results, will be joining us on Amazon.

The road is not easy, but let us tell you that it is very rewarding. The strategies outlined in this book will not only help you succeed on Amazon, they will also prevent that success from being taken from you overnight.

If you found this book useful and want to reach out to us, or if you have questions, you can shoot us an email at support@ecomcrew.com.

Thanks once again for reading this book. We wish you nothing but the best of success in your business.

And as always, happy selling.

Resources

You can find all the resources mentioned in this book below:

ClickFunnels templates

Amazon Optin Template
https://www.ecomcrew.com/optinfunnel

Contest Give-away Template
https://www.ecomcrew.com/giveawayfunnel

Product Sales Template
https://www.ecomcrew.com/salesfunnel

Amazon Coupon Optin Template
https://www.ecomcrew.com/amazonoptinfunnel

You'll need a ClickFunnels account before you can access these templates. If you don't have an account yet, you can use our affiliate link (it will help EcomCrew, at no cost to you): www.ecomcrew.com/clickfunnels

Listing image templates

Template1-Light.zip
https://www.ecomcrew.com/photography-light

Template2-Dark.zip
https://www.ecomcrew.com/photography-dark

Email swipe files

Email_Swipe_Files.docx
https://www.ecomcrew.com/swipefilesdoc

Email_Swipe_Files.pdf
https://www.ecomcrew.com/swipefilespdf

About the Authors

Mike Jackness

Mike has been involved in online marketing for over 10 years. During the poker craze of the early 2000s, he ran one of the largest poker affiliate companies in the world with over 60 employees (he even owned part of the Canadian Poker Tour!). After Black Friday (the day congress basically made it illegal for Americans to gamble online) he ventured into ecommerce with Treadmill.com. He sold that company in 2014 and have since then started multiple other ecommerce brands with total revenues over $7 million annually. Today he's based in San Diego but he's lived throughout the world including Las Vegas, the Cayman Islands, and out of a Class A motorhome while touring North America.

Dave Bryant

Dave is based in Vancouver, Canada but for nearly half of his life he has been involved with business in China. He formally ran the website ChineseImporting.com before it merged with EcomCrew in late 2017. In 2008 he started his company importing from China while finishing up his business degree at Simon Fraser University. By 2016 his company was doing approximately $2 million in revenue before he sold it for just under $1 million. He has another small startup in the oven as of 2017 focused, of course, on importing products from China. Oh yeah, he's also a former Amazon employee of 4 days.

About EcomCrew

If you've ever wondered: "Where can I find actionable ecommerce advice that gets results?", EcomCrew is the right place.

EcomCrew's mission is to publish content that is actually valuable to those seeking it out. During our ecommerce journey, we can't tell you how many times we've searched for answers to our questions and problems, only to end up in blogs that stop just short of answering them. Indeed, there are a lot of good blogs out there, but there are hundreds that only spew out fluff and are a total waste of time.

In the end we had to figure things out by ourselves. It was definitely a baptism by fire, but the end result was the necessary experience to build future stores from the ground up. We took this experience and turned it into a blog and podcast, hoping to help out entrepreneurs like ourselves who were looking for real and actionable business advice, not fluff and hot air.

As a result, EcomCrew has become a place where ecommerce business owners turn for proven ecommerce advice. Our transparent and results-focused approach to ecommerce is likely why we have grown our community to thousands of members in less than one year, with million dollar business owners subscribing to our email newsletter.

About EcomCrew Premium

Aside from the free content we provide, we also offer personalized attention and support you need to build a successful ecommerce brand.

EcomCrew Premium is a subscription-based membership to an exclusive group of ecommerce sellers. As a member, you get unlimited access to 1 on 1 support from Mike, Dave, and the entire EcomCrew to help you avoid making costly mistakes and prevent you from getting stuck on problems.

In addition, you get access to the following:
- Four full length courses including Import from China Like a Pro, Develop a 7 Figure Brand, Facebook Messenger for Ecommerce, and Launching a New Amazon Best Seller (the basis of this book)
- Access to all courses we plan on launching in the future
- Exclusive monthly webinars with million dollar ecommerce sellers as guests
- Exclusive monthly Q&A sessions where you can ask us anything
- Access to nearly a dozen conference webinars and presentations
- Access to an exclusive Facebook group

We normally only open registrations a couple of times per year, but if you've read this book and want to become a member, we have a special link set up for you:

www.ecomcrew.com/premium-book

Where to Find Us

EcomCrew website - **www.ecomcrew.com**

EcomCrew blog - **www.ecomcrew.com/blog**

The EcomCrew Podcast - **www.ecomcrew.com/ecomcrew-podcast**

Facebook page - **www.facebook.com/ecomcrew**

Facebook Premium group - **www.facebook.com/groups/ecomcrew**

YouTube channel - **www.youtube.com/ecomcrew**

Email - **support@ecomcrew.com**

Made in the USA
Columbia, SC
24 June 2019